CAN YOU SPOT BLACKBEARD'S TREASURE?

AN INTERACTIVE TREASURE ADVENTURE

BY THOMAS KINGSLEY TROUPE

CAPSTONE PRESS
a capstone imprint

Published by Capstone Press, an imprint of Capstone
1710 Roe Crest Drive
North Mankato, Minnesota 56003
capstonepub.com

Library of Congress Cataloging-in-Publication Data is
available on the Library of Congress website.
ISBN 9781669032007 (library binding)
ISBN 9781669031970 (paperback)
ISBN 9781669031987 (ebook PDF)

Summary: Spanish gold has been found on the North Carolina coast. Your mind
begins to race. Through your studies, you know the infamous pirate Blackbeard
was active in that area in the 1700s. But after his death in 1718, nobody knows what
happened to his hoard of gold. Could this be the first clue to finding his long-lost
treasure? It's up to you to find out! Will the choices YOU make help you dig up
Blackbeard's lost riches, or lead you to your doom?

Editorial Credits
Editor: Aaron Sautter; Designer: Bobbie Nuytten; Media Researcher:
Rebekah Hubstenberger; Production Specialist: Whitney Schaefer

Photo Credits
Alamy: GL Archive, 103, Pat & Chuck Blackley, 73; Bridgeman Images: Peter
Newark Historical Pictures, 12; Getty Images: Amana Images Inc, 28, Archive
Photos, 68, bopardau, 56, Hulton Archive, 100, i_7amza/500px, 92, iStock/
Kateryna Stremedlovs'ka, 59, iStock/studiocasper, 6, Noel Hendrickson, 42,
pixalot, 66, Stanislaw Pytel, 50; Shutterstock: Andrey_Kuzmin, design element
(map), Artem Mazunov, 95, ButtermilkgirlVirginia, 23, Fer Gregory, cover
(chest), jadimages, 87, John Piekos, 33, Krasula, 81, Leonardo Gonzalez, cover
(background), 1 (background), n_defender, 27, Net Vector, design element (light),
ValterDesign, 106, design element, (skull crossbones), zhekakopylov, 106-107; The
New York Public Library: Rare Book Division, 9

TABLE OF CONTENTS

About Your Adventure................5

CHAPTER 1
The Hunt Is On! 7

CHAPTER 2
Isle of Adventure 13

CHAPTER 3
Creepy Cave Captain 43

CHAPTER 4
Landlubber's Loot..................69

CHAPTER 5
A Pirate's Life and Death 101

Blackbeard Timeline....................105
More Plundering Pirates.................106
Other Paths to Explore 108
Bibliography 109
Glossary...............................110
Read More..............................111
Internet Sites.........................111
About the Author 112

ABOUT YOUR ADVENTURE

YOU are an international treasure hunter. When you're not running the city museum full- time, you spend your time searching for some of the most famous artifacts known to man.

One of the legendary finds you've always wanted to discover is the treasure of the dreaded pirate, Blackbeard. You'd love to display his riches at the museum one day! Will you be able to track down the pirate's long-lost booty?

Chapter One sets the scene. Then you choose which path to read. Follow the directions at the bottom of the page as you read the stories. The decisions you make will change your outcome. After you finish one path, go back and read the others for new perspectives and more adventures.

Turn the page to begin your adventure.

Gold doubloon coins were commonly used in Spanish colonies. Today, each coin would be worth more than 360 U.S. dollars.

CHAPTER 1

THE HUNT IS ON!

You're relaxing at home watching TV with your dog, Zeke. He's helping you eat popcorn while you flip through channels. You stop a moment to watch a news story.

"A local fisherman in North Carolina has found what appears to be a gold doubloon," the reporter on TV says.

"I pushed my boat offshore and there it was," an older fisherman explains. "Right there in the sand, all shiny and golden."

"Well, that seems to be the best catch of the day," the reporter jokes.

As the fisherman holds up the gold piece, you move closer to the TV to get a better look.

Turn the page.

"Those look like Spanish markings," you whisper to Zeke. "Blackbeard was a big problem for Spanish ships carrying gold back to Spain."

Could this be a piece of Blackbeard's treasure? you wonder.

You've studied a lot about the Golden Age of Piracy. You know that Blackbeard's real name was Edward Teach. He was a privateer for the British government. It's believed Teach plundered Spanish ships during the War of Spanish Succession. He later became a pirate full-time. He formed his own crew and kept the riches he found for himself.

You watch the rest of the story. Blackbeard isn't mentioned, but you're excited. Could this be the first real clue that Blackbeard's treasure exists?

In your studies, you've discovered several places where Blackbeard's treasure might be found. His ship, *Queen Anne's Revenge*, ran aground off the coast of North Carolina in 1718. The wreck was found in 1996. A number of cannons, artifacts, and even a large anchor were recovered, but no treasure was discovered.

Turn the page.

Edward Teach, also known as the fearsome pirate Blackbeard

After *Queen Anne's Revenge* was beached, Blackbeard tried to live a normal life in North Carolina as Edward Teach. He was pardoned by Governor Charles Eden and lived in a house in Plum Point. It's possible that he hid his treasure there.

A short time later, Blackbeard and his crew boarded a smaller ship from his fleet called *Adventure*. The sea was calling Teach back to the pirate life. Not long after his return to piracy, Blackbeard went down with the *Adventure* near Ocracoke Island.

There are caves and many places to hide treasure near the island. But nothing has been found there yet. You wonder if it ever will be.

You bend down to pet Zeke, who's eyeing the bowl of popcorn on the coffee table. He wags his tail and barks at you.

"What if Blackbeard hid the treasure in the Caribbean before coming to North Carolina?" you ask Zeke, not expecting an answer. Your dog barks again. He probably wants you to take him for a w-a-l-k.

Blackbeard seized a lot of valuables while terrorizing the Cayman Islands in the Caribbean. He could've dumped his treasure there somewhere, hoping to return and claim it one day.

Other treasure hunters are probably planning their trips right now. If you want to find Blackbeard's treasure first, you'd better get moving!

To search the coast of Ocracoke Island, turn to page 13.

To explore caves in the Cayman Islands, turn to page 43.

To visit Blackbeard's North Carolina home, turn to page 69.

Blackbeard's final battle took place on November 22, 1718.

CHAPTER 2

ISLE OF ADVENTURE

It's decided! You plan to head to Ocracoke Island, off the coast of North Carolina. Blackbeard and his band of pirates hid out there to attack any passing ships that came in and out of port.

It's also the site where the dreaded pirate was attacked, beheaded, and went down with his ship. You've heard stories that Blackbeard's headless body swam around the ship a few times before he finally sank under the sea. You're not sure that's true, but it sure adds to the infamous pirate's legend!

On the way to the island, you stop and talk with the fisherman who found the doubloon. He tells you his name is Jack and shows you his find proudly, scratching his gray beard.

Turn the page.

As you look closely at the coin, you can confirm that it's from a Spanish galleon. But it doesn't provide any other clues.

"I'm looking for more of these," you say, raising the gold coin. "A whole lot of them. A pirate's bounty worth."

"Well, you're not alone," Jack says. "Ever since that news story aired, people have been combing the beach with those metal-finder things. I guess they're all hoping to find gold, too."

You realize Jack means metal detectors. You smile, since you brought your own detector too, just in case.

You study the doubloon again. Could it be a piece from Blackbeard's long-lost treasure? It might be useful to have a local resident with you for the hunt. So, you invite Jack to join you.

"I guess I could tag along," he says, taking his gold piece back. "I wouldn't mind catching a few more of these!"

You scan the beach and look toward Ocracoke Island. In the distance, you can see the lighthouse you read about on the plane ride here. Getting to the top of the beacon might provide a good view of the island and help you decide where to search.

To visit the lighthouse on Ocracoke Island, turn to page 16.

To scour the beach with your metal detector, turn to page 19.

"Do you feel like going to the lighthouse?" you ask Jack.

"You don't think that treasure is in there, do you?" he asks.

"No," you admit. "If it was, someone would have found it by now. I just want to get a nice view of the island from up there. Maybe we'll see a good spot to explore."

The old guy shrugs and nods as if he doesn't really care either way.

As you approach the tall white lighthouse, you can see a few windows along the side. You're surprised that there aren't more cars nearby. You half expected a line of tourists waiting to explore the lighthouse for themselves.

You spot a plaque near the lighthouse that gives a brief history. As you begin reading it, one sentence makes you groan:

The lighthouse is owned and maintained by the United States Coast Guard and is closed to the public.

"Perfect," you say sarcastically. You already feel like you're wasting your time.

"I should have mentioned that," Jack says. "Sorry, it's been a while since I've been out this way."

As you get ready to turn and leave, you notice a uniformed woman coming out a door at the bottom of the lighthouse. She turns around as if to lock the door.

"Hello!" you shout. "Can I ask a favor?"

The woman is from the Coast Guard. Her badge lets you know she's Lieutenant Collins. You explain who you are and give her some information about your museum back home.

Turn the page.

After a few minutes, you ask if you can go to the top for just a few minutes to look around.

Lieutenant Collins looks doubtful at first. But then she quickly motions for you to come in. The three of you climb the spiral metal stairs inside the lighthouse to the top. Thankfully, you see that the light is turned off. You step out onto the observation deck and scan the horizon.

On the deck you can see beaches and rocky inlets nearby. Further north you can see wooded areas. Unfortunately, nothing sticks out as an obvious spot to hide pirate treasure.

Jack looks at the sea. It seems like he wants to go back to fishing. You thank Lieutenant Collins and climb back down the long spiral steps.

Turn to page 22.

Combing the beach with your trusty metal detector seems like a great place to start. You might find another doubloon or some clues to where the treasure is hidden. You retrieve the detector from your rental car and head to the sandy beach. You notice a few other people have the same idea, just as Jack said.

"Where did you find your doubloon?" you ask. Jack leads you to the shore's edge near some docks.

"I dug around here a bit, thinking I'd find another," Jack says, tugging at his beard. "But no luck, I'm afraid."

You switch on your device and begin scanning the sands, hoping to pick up on something. After about a half hour, the metal detector starts making noise. There's something down there!

Turn the page.

You squat down, pull out a small pocket spade from your pack, and begin digging. After a while, the tip of your spade strikes something solid. You quickly clear the sand away to reveal a glint of silver. You feel a rush of excitement as you reach down to pull out the treasure!

It's a spoon.

"Could this be from Blackbeard's ship?" you wonder out loud.

"Nup," Jack says. "This is from Dave's Diner down the road. See the *D* on the handle?"

You sigh and start scanning the sand with your detector again.

While you do, Jack casts a line from the beach with his fishing rod. The guy just can't resist fishing. It's just as well since you've only got one metal detector.

You scan up and down the beach, hoping to find something hidden in the sand. After another twenty minutes, the detector starts making noise again. You dig into the sand but stick your finger with an old fishhook. Later, you find a broken pocket watch from the 1980s and an old soup can.

It was worth a try, but you won't find Blackbeard's treasure this way. As you put your metal detector away, you realize that Blackbeard wouldn't bury his treasure out in the open. Anyone walking along the shore could find it. Blackbeard was smart, dangerous, and paranoid. He'd definitely find a place no one, not even his own crew, would expect to find his treasure.

Turn the page.

You get the feeling you're just wasting time and decide to head to Ocracoke Village. In your studies of the infamous pirate, you've learned that Blackbeard's second ship, *Adventure,* was sunk off the coast of the village.

You get the feeling that Blackbeard might have dumped his treasure before his last stand. Sailing the seas as a pirate with all of your riches would be kind of foolhardy. Then again, Blackbeard was taken by surprise. It's possible he was transporting his treasure to another site when he was attacked.

Jack suggests using his boat to go to the spot where Blackbeard supposedly met his demise. You could easily dive below the water and explore the site yourself.

Blackbeard was smart. Some claimed he told people his treasure "lay in a location known only to him and the devil."

Thick woods on Ocracoke Island

You wonder if his booty is even close to the sea at all. It's possible that he hid it somewhere no one would suspect. You look over and see the dense woods on the eastern end of the island. Could the pirate have hidden his booty there? It was close enough to his home, but far enough away from spying eyes.

To take the boat out to where the *Adventure* sank, turn to page 24.

To explore the nearby woods, turn to page 26.

If you can pinpoint where the *Adventure* went down, maybe you can find the treasure at the bottom of the sea.

"Let's take the boat out," you decide. "I want to dive down and see if I can spot anything."

Jack seems excited to get back out on the water. While he goes to get his boat, you rent some scuba gear in town.

As you wait for Jack, you notice a tourist attraction called Blackbeard's Floating Museum. It's just a fake pirate ship anchored in the bay. It doesn't seem to be going anywhere and won't interfere with your search. Tourists are gathered on board, listening to people dressed as pirates. There are cannons on the deck that don't quite look like the kind Blackbeard would have had.

You wander into the museum gift shop. Inside, you glance at a display of souvenir maps for sale. The maps aren't much help, but you're sure the kids love them. You are almost certain the ship sank somewhere close by, but you're unsure of the exact spot. When Jack arrives, he guides the boat to a spot less than a mile off the coast.

"Here we be," Jack says, killing the engine. "This is where ol' Beardy was thought to have met his fate."

He turns on a depth scanner and points to the screen. You're itching to dive in and explore. But maybe you should see how deep you need to go first.

To jump in and start exploring, turn to page 28.

To use Jack's depth scanner first, turn to page 30.

You think there's no way that Blackbeard would have kept his treasure aboard his ship. You know that Blackbeard used to wait for other ships to approach before attacking them. He likely hid his treasure in a place where he could watch for ships while keeping an eye on his riches. You decide to explore the woods and see what you can find.

As you drive to the lush part of the island, you spot an old woman selling things in front of her home. You decide to stop and see what she has. Maybe you can find a clue about the treasure.

The woman points to a book that looks as old as anything in your museum. When you open it, you see the name *EDWARD* scrawled inside the front cover. Tucked between the pages is an old piece of paper. It looks like a treasure map!

Treasure maps are popular in many books and movies about pirates. But they rarely buried their treasure and didn't use maps to find it.

In your years of study, you've learned that pirates didn't leave maps to their treasure. It's a myth used in stories and movies. Even so, the map makes you curious. Could this one be the exception?

To leave the book and keep searching, turn to page 32.

To buy the book and follow the treasure map, turn to page 34.

You strap on your scuba gear and take the plunge. It's been a while since you last went diving. But after years of training, it's like riding a bike. You head toward the ocean floor. Before you get too deep, you hear something rumble.

The water is about 30 feet (9 meters) deep off the shore of Ocracoke Island.

As you swim toward the surface, something big and round drops past you, plummeting to the bottom of the sea. It almost looks like a cannonball. When you get to the surface, you see Jack's boat has been destroyed. The poor guy is floating in the water like a dead fish.

Was that tourist attraction using REAL cannonballs? you wonder. *Did they really not see us out here?*

You can't believe that fake pirate ship would do something as dangerous as firing cannonballs into the sea. They've sunk Jack's boat. Before you can start to swim back to shore, another cannonball flies straight at you. Your treasure hunt is over, and now you're food for the fish.

THE END

To follow another path, turn to page 11.
To learn more about Blackbeard, turn to page 101.

You gaze at Jack's depth scanner, but you're not sure what you're seeing. He points to some small shapes drifting by and identifies them as fish.

"We're not here to fish," you remind him. "We're looking for treasure."

Jack smiles and nods, then points out a spot below that the fish seem to be avoiding.

"That there is a haunted depth," he tells you. "No fish will swim there."

"You think there's something down there, spooking the fish?" you ask.

"Seems to be," Jack says. "Could be your pirate buddy's rich stuff."

You don't believe in curses or hauntings but decide it's worth checking out.

As you begin putting on your diving gear, you hear an explosion off the coast. You and Jack turn to see puffs of smoke from the tourist ship's cannons.

"Uh-oh," Jack grunts. "Bad place to park."

The fake pirate ship's cannons must be real! They fired them to entertain the tourists. They must not have seen your small boat out here.

The cannonballs hit and blast the small boat to bits. Your hunt for pirate gold has come to a sudden end.

THE END

To follow another path, turn to page 11.
To learn more about Blackbeard, turn to page 101.

You know treasure maps don't exist. Plus, there were probably more than a few people named Edward that lived in the area. There's no proof that the book or map belonged to Blackbeard, also known as Edward Teach. You thank the woman for showing you the book and move on.

You and Jack continue along the dirt road to the coast. Jack tells you which areas of the coast are deep enough for a ship to get close to without running aground. It was likely the *Adventure* got close to land to hide from approaching ships.

Blackbeard may also have sent small boats to shore with a little bit of his treasure at a time. He may have then killed the men when they returned to keep the location secret. Even so, the hidden spot would have to be somewhere that was easily reached from the ocean.

Looking up, you see there are hills in the distance. They would make good lookouts and possibly places to hide treasure.

You also spot a cave that's somewhat hidden by vines and overgrown brush. Could Blackbeard and his crew have rowed a small boat into the cave?

A small sea cave

To explore the watery cave, turn to page 36.
To search the hills along the coast, turn to page 37.

Can't hurt to try, you think and buy the old book and map from the woman.

"Thank ye kindly," she cackles as she puts the money into an old cigar box.

You and Jack head to the coastline and unfold the map. Using the coast and the old road as reference points, you discover the starting point on the map isn't far from where you're standing.

Following the path scrawled on the map, you come across different markers along the way. The windy route leads you to a cluster of three boulders, then through a swampy area, and then to a clearing where some strange blue flowers are growing.

You look through the tall grass until you see that someone has made an X with a bunch of white rocks.

"*X* marks the spot," you tell Jack. He nods but doesn't seem overly excited about your find.

You pull out your collapsible spade and start digging. After about fifteen minutes, you hit something hard and metallic. Excited, you dig faster until you uncover a rusty old coffee can from the 1970s. You open it up and find about thirty dirt-crusted pennies and two old nickels. You've found treasure, all right—just not the one you hoped for. This looks like it belonged to a boy named Edward, not Edward Teach, a.k.a. Blackbeard.

THE END

To follow another path, turn to page 11.
To learn more about Blackbeard, turn to page 101.

You and Jack wade into the watery cave to explore what's inside. Hacking through the overgrowth, you find a small room.

Jack doesn't want to go any deeper. "I'm not much for small spaces. I think I'm gonna stay here."

You venture further into the dark room. About twenty feet in, you stop and gasp. There, lit by your flashlight, is a small pile of treasure. But as you reach for it, you hear a creak and a wooden snap. Before you know it, the entrance to the room has caved in behind you.

You shout out for Jack but hear no response. You can only hope he wasn't buried and is going for help. You found some of Blackbeard's treasure. Sadly, you may not live to prove it.

THE END

To follow another path, turn to page 11.
To learn more about Blackbeard, turn to page 101.

You don't have a good feeling about that cave. When you look at it again, it almost looks like a skull with a mouth, drinking in the ocean. It seems like a bad sign, and you decide to look elsewhere.

You set out for the hills instead. After about twenty minutes, you look up and see a strange rock formation. It almost looks like the rocks have . . . horns? You take a step closer to look, and your feet sink into the ground. Luckily, you catch yourself before falling through the sinkhole that's opened under you. Then you hear the sound of rocks falling and the *tink, tink* of something metallic.

With Jack's help, you pull yourself out of the sinkhole. You tie some fishing line to a flashlight and lower it into the hole. Within moments, you can see the unmistakable glint of gold.

"We've found it!" you cry.

Turn the page.

You resist the urge to jump up and down in excitement. After all, you're not sure just how stable the ground is here.

You remember that Blackbeard was once quoted as saying, "The location is known only to me and the devil." Maybe the horned rock formation was a clue?

More importantly, how do you safely get down to the treasure?

To have Jack lower you into the sinkhole, go to page 39.

To tie a rope to a tree and lower yourself down, turn to page 40.

Jack has caught all kinds of huge fish. He's probably stronger than he looks. You ask him to help and then tie a rope around your waist as he ties the other end around himself. Holding your flashlight, you descend into the depths.

As you get closer, something rumbles below you. You urge Jack to lower you more quickly. You can see that the treasure is falling through another hole like sand in an hourglass.

You finally reach the shrinking pile and blindly reach out and grab something. Sadly, you watch as the last of the treasure sifts into the giant hole. You look down to see what you've grabbed. It appears to be the skull of one of Blackbeard's doomed crewmen. No treasure for you. Just a reminder of Blackbeard's cruelty.

THE END

To follow another path, turn to page 11.
To learn more about Blackbeard, turn to page 101.

You decide to tie a rope to a tree and lower yourself down. Jack looks relieved. He doesn't seem to be a fan of small spaces. As you drop lower into the hole, you can see the treasure getting closer and closer. When you reach the bottom, you find a decent pile of gold doubloons, jewels, and old artifacts.

Is this all of it? You can't help but think there should be more, especially with how much Blackbeard stole during his pirating days.

Looking around, you're not sure how Blackbeard and his crew got the treasure into this hidden vault. And you don't know how you'll get it out either.

As you get ready to untie the rope, the ground below you starts to rumble and shake. Leaning forward, you quickly scoop up a handful of doubloons, a golden goblet, and a jeweled necklace.

Just then, the treasure is literally sucked down into another sinkhole far below you. You can only dangle from the rope over the gaping pit and helplessly watch the rich stuff disappear into the earth.

You're not sure where it went or if it will ever be found. All you know is you got your hands on a little chunk of Blackbeard's treasure. The museum back home is going to be more popular than ever!

THE END

To follow another path, turn to page 11.
To learn more about Blackbeard, turn to page 101.

Little Cayman Island

CHAPTER 3

CREEPY CAVE CAPTAIN

You have a feeling that Blackbeard wouldn't risk dragging his hoard of treasure back to North Carolina. In fact, he may have even avoided hiding his treasure on Ocracoke Island.

For that matter, nobody even knows for sure if the doubloon the fisherman found belonged to Blackbeard. It could have been from anywhere.

"I'm going to the Cayman Islands," you tell Zeke. "Even if I don't find anything, it'll be a nice vacation."

You make plans for your dog to stay with your sister and promise him you'll come back with something nice and shiny.

Turn the page.

You think about Edward Teach and his transformation from privateer to pirate. He likely decided that stealing for the British government wasn't worthwhile. Why do all the work just to hand over the treasure to someone else?

Blackbeard captured a French merchant ship and converted it into a 40-gun warship. Then he renamed it *Queen Anne's Revenge*. He assembled a crew of about 300 men to help him on his quest to rule the waters.

Blackbeard made himself into a scary figure while terrorizing the Caribbean. With his huge, bushy beard and wild eyes, he was described as looking almost demonic.

He was also said to stick lit fuses into his hair and beard so smoke rose up around his face. This made him look even scarier. He carried multiple guns and wore velvet clothes and colored silks.

You book a ticket for the Cayman Islands to search the area where the pirate was most active. From the research you've done, you know that Blackbeard staged his raids from two islands in the Caymans: Cayman Brac and Little Cayman.

Cayman Brac is a larger and more populated island. You learn there are caves there. There may be a cave large enough to hold a pirate's fortune.

Little Cayman is smaller. Not as many people live there. It's possible Blackbeard hid his treasure there, where no one might see him do it.

To explore Cayman Brac, turn to page 46.
To explore Little Cayman, turn to page 47.

Cayman Brac, here I come, you think.

You think the larger island could be a likely place for Blackbeard to hide his pile of treasure. With all the caves on the island, it's hard to imagine a better place to stash loads of gold.

After arriving, you read more about the caves and learn there are guided tours through them. To get a feel for the types of caves Blackbeard might have used, you sign up for a tour.

The tour guide is a local guy named Kingston. He gives a bit of history on the area as he leads the group through the caves. Along the way, you spot several passages that people aren't allowed to explore.

Could the treasure be hidden in one of those passages? you wonder.

To finish the tour with the group, turn to page 49.

To sneak away from the group to explore, turn to page 51.

"I'm going to visit the little guy," you decide. Exploring Little Cayman seems like the right choice. The smaller island won't be as crowded as Cayman Brac. You doubt other would-be treasure hunters are looking there.

When you arrive, you're amazed by how tiny the island is. Unlike Cayman Brac, there aren't a lot of actual caves on the island. Instead, you discover there's a small underwater cluster of coral known as Cumber's Caves near Blossom Village. You wonder if the pirate could have buried his treasure underwater. It would be a lot harder for any landlubbers to find it that way.

When you arrive in Blossom Village, you rent some diving gear and a small boat so you can look for yourself. You head further off the coast until you find Cumber's Caves. The water is a peaceful, clear blue. It seems impossible that a fierce pirate like Blackbeard once roamed these calm waters.

Turn the page.

Off in the distance is a boat with a large crew of men who are watching you. You wave, but the men don't wave back.

After gearing up, you make the dive. The coral wall is beautiful. You see turtles, a stingray, and more colorful fish than you can count. You dive down toward a small cave formed in the coral. While swimming through the cave opening, you cut your arm on a sharp edge of coral. The cut is bleeding quite a bit, but it doesn't seem too serious.

To return to the surface to tend to your wound, turn to page 53.

To keep exploring the cave, turn to page 55.

You paid for the tour, so you decide you might as well get your money's worth. Kingston talks about bats and how the temperature changes the deeper into the caves you go. He's right. It's much cooler than it is outside and it's almost chilly in places. He explains the difference between stalactites and stalagmites. He points out that stalactites are on the ceiling, while stalagmites are on the ground.

As you and the group progress through the cave, you keep noticing the passages that aren't part of the tour. You really wish you could see what, if anything, is in those areas.

When the tour is finally over, you end up in the cave's gift shop. You consider buying a keychain with a picture of the cave on it but decide against it. You notice that Kingston is standing near the exit, thanking people for coming by.

Turn the page.

The Cayman Islands are home to many caves. A few are open for tourists to visit, but most are closed to the public.

You wonder if you could get a private tour and explore some of the passages that weren't part of the public tour. Maybe you can convince Kingston to let you in there or at least show you around? Or you could try to sneak into the caves after the tours are closed for the day. It's risky, but what else would a treasure hunter do?

To sneak into the caves by yourself, turn to page 57.

To ask Kingston to show you other parts of the cave, turn to page 58.

The tour is interesting, but you're not here to learn about bats and cave formations. You're here to find Blackbeard's treasure. To do that, you'll need to break a few rules.

During part of the tour, Kingston turns off all the lights in the cave. You take the opportunity to sneak away. You feel your way around in the dark until you can hear the group move on.

Once the coast is clear, you turn on your flashlight and head back toward the first passage you were shown. But after a while, nothing looks familiar to you. You wonder if you've wandered too far into the caves. The more you explore, the more lost you become.

You stop and listen, hoping to hear the rest of the tour group. Five minutes go by, and you hear absolutely nothing. The cave is as quiet as a tomb. Your heart beats harder as you realize this place might actually become your tomb.

Turn the page.

As you frantically run around looking for the exit, you take a bad step. The next thing you know, you've slid down a slick passageway and fall more than ten feet into another chamber. One of your legs is broken. You cry out for help, but you're too deep in the caves for anyone to hear you. Weeks pass before your body is found, dead from hunger and thirst.

THE END

To follow another path, turn to page 11.
To learn more about Blackbeard, turn to page 101.

It's not a great idea to swim in the ocean with blood coming from your arm. As much as you hate to do it, you swim to the surface and find some visitors on your boat. They look like the men in the boat you saw earlier. None of them look friendly. They grab you and roughly pull you out of the water as they shout at you.

You don't understand what they're saying. But you swear you hear the words "pirate" and "treasure" somewhere in there. Hoping to show them you're not a threat, you raise your hands in surrender. You notice one of them is holding a long knife, almost as big as a sword. Some of the others have guns.

Before you can explain what you're doing, they stab you in the stomach. As you lay bleeding, they take you out to sea and dump you in the middle of the ocean. You watch helplessly as they motor away, leaving you on your own. You don't even know which direction the coast is.

Turn the page.

You had hoped to simply bandage the cut on your arm and keep looking for the treasure. Now you're seriously wounded and have no way of returning to shore.

You know that even if you don't drown or bleed to death, the sharks will surely finish you off. Just like Blackbeard's treasure, you'll probably never be found.

THE END

To follow another path, turn to page 11.
To learn more about Blackbeard, turn to page 101.

The cut on your arm doesn't seem too bad. And you don't want to lose track of the places you've already searched. Despite the stinging pain in your arm, you swim on. Little trails of blood flow from your arm with every movement. As you explore the small cave in the coral, you see a glimpse of something golden in the sand below. You pause for a moment and stare at the space. Maybe you're just seeing things?

Then a crab walks by, shifting some of the sand away. There's definitely some gold down there!

Excited, you swim down and brush the sand away. You find a golden plate that looks old. You reach down and pull it up from the sand, certain it came from Blackbeard's treasure. You dig a little deeper and find more gold doubloons, silver goblets, and jewelry. You're convinced that if you keep digging, you'll find even more loot.

Turn the page.

Tiger sharks are usually 10 to 14 feet (3 to 4.3 m) long and can weigh as much as 1,400 pounds (635 kilograms.)

I've done it! you think to yourself. *I found Blackbeard's treasure!*

As you pump your fist in excitement, a tiger shark clamps down on your arm. You try to reach for something to fight the beast off, but the shark pulls you away to be its next meal.

THE END

To follow another path, turn to page 11.
To learn more about Blackbeard, turn to page 101.

You're pretty sure there's no way the tour guide will break the rules for you. So, you'll have to sneak into the caves yourself after the place is closed.

That night, you carefully sneak toward the cave entrance. But before you can enter, you hear footsteps and whistling in the distance. You hide in some nearby bushes. Soon, a guard walks around the cave tour building. She hasn't seen you, so if you're quiet, you can probably slip in without much trouble.

As you pass through the entrance, you see a sign with a map. It shows the passages and route that the tour goes through. You could take a picture of it with your phone to help you find your way. But do you have enough time before the guard returns?

To risk being discovered and take a photo of the map, turn to page 60.

To forget the map and head into the caves, turn to page 61.

It would be unwise and dangerous to explore the caves on your own. You approach Kingston and introduce yourself. You tell him about your museum that you run back home and explain why you're here. He seems interested in helping you. Giving him a giant tip doesn't hurt either.

Kingston agrees to meet you at the caves at dusk after the tours are closed for the day. The two of you venture into the caves, and he shows you some of the passages he and the tour guides have gone through.

"Most of these passages are dead ends," Kingston says.

When you get to a narrow passage, Kingston tells you there is a ledge along one wall called "the plank." The ledge is very thin and almost impossible to navigate. Even worse, it's above a deep section of the cave. If you fell, you would most likely be killed.

Narrow passages in caves can be tricky and dangerous.

Kingston warns you that it's far too dangerous to attempt. If people are too afraid to explore "the plank," this could be the perfect spot for a hidden treasure.

"I think we should look deeper into the cave," Kingston says. "But you're the treasure hunter. I can see you want to try."

To walk "the plank" and see if the treasure is inside, turn to page 62.

To move deeper into the cave, turn to page 64.

If you're quick, the guard won't see you, right? You take a quick photo of the map and venture into the cave. Staying quiet, you follow the tourist path until you find the first "off-limits" passage the tour passed by.

As you crawl through the passage, you learn why tours aren't allowed. The space is small, and it makes you nervous to be in here. After following some twists and turns, you discover you are way off the tour path.

Eventually, you find yourself in a larger cave. In front of you is a small pile of gold pieces. They look like they could be from Blackbeard's time. You know it's not his entire treasure, but it's a start. You hope to find the rest of the treasure in these caves. Unless this is all that's left . . .

THE END

To follow another path, turn to page 11.
To learn more about Blackbeard, turn to page 101.

Though pirates use maps in movies and books, they didn't use them in real life—and neither will you. You set out and decide to go as far as you can before exploring some of the "off-limits" passages.

Some time later, you see a slope going deep into the ground. As you venture forward, you notice something golden in the light of your flashlight. Pulling away cobwebs, you see it's a golden goblet. There are rich jewels on the cup. You're excited and quickly grab the goblet.

But you don't see the ancient rope that's attached to the cup. Suddenly, you hear a click above you. As you look up, tons of gold and treasure dump down on you. For a moment, you can't believe your eyes. You've found Blackbeard's treasure hoard! But moments later, the weight of all that gold crushes the life from you.

THE END

To follow another path, turn to page 11.
To learn more about Blackbeard, turn to page 101.

You ignore Kingston's warning and decide to take your chances on "the plank." As you squeeze into the gap, you can see how it got its name. There is a large gorge with hundreds of stalagmites below. They point up like sharp daggers in the darkness. You slide carefully along the edge, looking down at your feet to make sure you don't step off the edge.

"Are you okay, treasure hunter?" Kingston calls out. "No one who has gone in there has come back."

I wish you would've said that before, you think. But you answer him with, "I'm fine so far! Just trying to concentrate."

After a couple slips and close calls, you find yourself much deeper into the chamber. You start to wonder if it was foolish to "walk the plank."

Further ahead, you spot a wooden platform suspended over the gorge. It's held in place by a series of old ropes. On the platform are some old wooden chests and boxes. Is the treasure inside?

Suddenly, the ledge beneath your feet crumbles. You have only seconds to react! You leap to the platform and climb up. The "plank" you were walking on has disintegrated and crumbled to the chasm below.

You take a moment to catch your breath and look at the boxes. But before you can open any of them, you hear the creak and strain of old ropes. A series of snaps follows as the ropes fail to support your weight.

Before you can react, you're dropping into the gorge along with the platform. You crash down to the pit of stalagmites along with the wooden chests. Glimmering gold doubloons bounce all around you before you close your eyes for the last time.

THE END

To follow another path, turn to page 11.
To learn more about Blackbeard, turn to page 101.

You hired Kingston for a reason, so it would be unwise not to follow his advice. You leave "the plank" for a more foolish treasure seeker.

Kingston leads you past where the tour ends and shows you the last few passages where visitors aren't allowed. But he tells you that most of the paths lead to dead ends. He shrugs and says that he and the other guides have been through all the passages and haven't found anything.

Feeling like you've wasted your time, you and your guide head back. As you do, you notice a large rock you hadn't noticed before. When you approach it, you can feel a cool wind blowing from around it. Kingston looks confused, but you convince him there's a passage back there. The rock is heavy, but you think the two of you could move it.

To move the rock and explore the passage behind it, go to page 65.

To call it quits and look for the treasure elsewhere, turn to page 67.

The rock is very heavy. But with willpower and your combined strength, the two of you roll the rock out of the way. When you do, the wind whips through—and a horrible stench follows. A moment later, a cluster of bats zips out of the hole, buzzing by your face and hair.

"Gross," you mutter, spitting out a tiny bat hair or two from your mouth.

When your heartbeat returns to normal, you crouch down and crawl through the passageway. It's damp. It stinks. And it's a tight squeeze. But you continue forward until you can stand again. As you sweep your flashlight around, you see there are bones along the sides of the passage.

You have a bad feeling as you keep moving to the end of the tunnel. There, you see a skeleton lying against the wall. It's wearing a hat that looks like it could've belonged to a pirate.

Turn the page.

A fancy sword has been jammed into the skeleton's ribcage. His bony hand holds a pen over a small, dusty journal.

You read the journal and discover the skeleton was one of Blackbeard's crew members. The dreaded pirate must have killed this man for betraying him and left his body here. The entry says something about Blackbeard quitting the pirate life and returning home. You didn't find Blackbeard's treasure. But you found his sword, and possibly an important clue that could lead to the pirate's hoard.

THE END

To follow another path, turn to page 11.
To learn more about Blackbeard, turn to page 101.

Nothing about the rock seems like it could be hiding any treasure. You can tell Kingston would rather leave the boulder where it is. It's starting to feel like you've wasted your time exploring the caves. They're just a place for tourists to visit. If the treasure was here, someone would have found it by now.

There are a bunch of other caves on the island. You spend the rest of your trip going on cave tours and secretly exploring passages. But you don't find anything except empty caverns, underground waterways, and lots of bat poop. Before you know it, your vacation is over. Looks like you're going home empty-handed.

THE END

To follow another path, turn to page 11.
To learn more about Blackbeard, turn to page 101.

Between 1717 and 1719, England's King George I offered to forgive pirates if they turned themselves in to authorities.

CHAPTER 4

LANDLUBBER'S LOOT

"If I were a pirate, I'd want to keep my treasure close to home," you tell Zeke, who wags his tail. "How would you keep an eye on it if it's too far away?"

You've done a lot of research on Blackbeard. Most people assume his treasure is hidden away in some cave or buried somewhere where *X* marks the spot.

It's hard to believe, but Blackbeard once retired from his pirating ways. He returned to life as Edward Teach after being pardoned by North Carolina governor Charles Eden in May 1718. This was shortly after he and his crew ran his ship, *Queen Anne's Revenge*, aground.

Turn the page.

Many pirates retired during this time. Britain's King George I issued a "Proclamation for Suppressing of Pirates" on September 5, 1717. If pirates turned themselves in, their crimes were forgiven. If they didn't surrender before July 1, 1719, they would be fair game for bounty hunters and cutthroats.

However, the king's proclamation said nothing about pirates turning over their plundered riches or goods. Knowing that, you think Blackbeard probably kept his plunder, but likely stashed it somewhere to keep it safe.

Many believe Blackbeard paid Charles Eden to protect him from others who wanted him dead. After receiving his pardon, Blackbeard lived in a small home near Plum Point, North Carolina. He also stayed in a place called the Hammock House. The house is still standing and has been since around 1700.

You know Blackbeard didn't stay at either location for long. But it might be worth investigating them both. There are plenty of "pirate tours" in the area, thanks to Blackbeard's fame. But a tour probably won't be much help. Checking these places out on your own makes more sense. The real question is, where do you start?

To investigate Hammock House, turn to page 72.

To find Blackbeard's home off the coast, turn to page 74.

Shortly after arriving in Bath, North Carolina, you ask around about the pirate and his life in the town. Most people tell you that Blackbeard's small home doesn't exist anymore. All that's left is some old stones from the foundation. If there was ever any treasure hidden in his old house, it's long gone.

You decide to visit Hammock House in Beaufort instead. Legend says that Blackbeard sometimes stayed there between voyages. Maybe he hid treasure there during his visits.

When you arrive at Hammock House, you find a beautiful white, two-story structure with a nice front porch. This building is said to be one of the oldest in the state. It once served as an inn, but today it's a private home.

As you admire the building, a nearby tour group walks by. You hear the guide explain that Blackbeard stayed there on occasion.

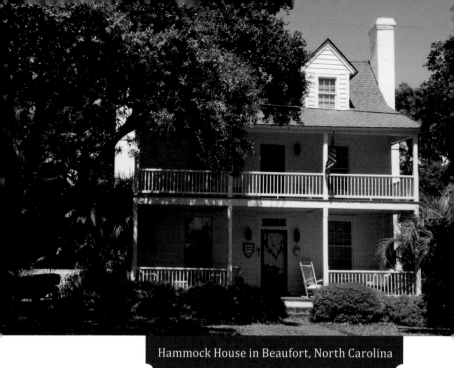

Hammock House in Beaufort, North Carolina

You'd love to get inside and see if there are any clues. If it's as old as they say, chances are good that the old house could hold a pirate treasure—just waiting to be found! However, people live there now, and it's not open to the public. How can you get inside?

To sneak into the house when the owners aren't there, turn to page 76.

To ask the people living there if you can investigate, turn to page 78.

After you arrive in Bath, North Carolina, you learn that the home Blackbeard lived in is no longer standing. Even so, you want to see the site. Maybe you can find a useful clue there. You just hope you're not wasting your time.

After talking with some locals, you meet Cathy, who works at the local bakery. She knows the location of Blackbeard's old house and points you in the right direction.

"You think I could come along?" Cathy asks. "I love that old pirate stuff."

"Sure," you reply. "It'd be nice to have a local show me around."

When you and Cathy get to the site, you see there's not much left. Only a few blocks from the foundation lie on the ground. Most of the area is completely overgrown. You pull out your trusty shovel, and Cathy shakes her head.

"You should probably get permission to dig here first," Cathy says. "I don't want us to get in trouble."

You realize she's right. It's not just some abandoned lot you're digging into, but a historic site. However, if you ask for permission, the city could say no. Otherwise, you could just search elsewhere.

To ask permission to dig there, turn to page 80.

To search other areas of Bath for clues, turn to page 82.

You're not a criminal. Breaking into the house is against the law. Although you know it's wrong, you tell yourself it's for the good of history. Blackbeard's treasure should be discovered and displayed in a museum, not hidden in some old house!

Feeling like a secret agent on a stakeout, you watch the house for a few nights. Amazingly, the people living there don't seem to go anywhere. When they finally do leave, you quickly run up to the house and stand in front of the door. As you reach for the doorknob, you feel your heart beat like a drum inside your chest.

Am I really going to break into someone's home? you ask yourself.

You take a deep breath. You need to know if the treasure is inside. As you prepare to break and enter, you hear a low growl to your left. A massive dog with saliva dripping off its face is watching you.

"Nice doggie," you whisper and slowly back away.

The dog barks as if to say: *Intruder! Get out of here!*

You sprint from the house back to your rental car. You jump into the car, breathing heavily. What were you thinking? Were you really going to break the law just on a hunch?

You go back to your hotel and plan your trip back home. It's probably for the best— before you get into real trouble.

THE END

To follow another path, turn to page 11.
To learn more about Blackbeard, turn to page 101.

You know from experience that sometimes the best way to get something done is to just ask permission. You approach the house and notice there appears to be a crawl space under the front porch.

That's curious. I wonder why that's there? you think to yourself.

You shrug your shoulders and ring the doorbell. A man and woman answer the door and greet you with a puzzled look.

"Can we help you?" the woman asks.

You learn that the people living here are Bill and Verna Williams. You introduce yourself and explain that you operate a museum back home and are interested in finding Blackbeard's treasure. They nod politely, but they seem confident you won't find anything. Thankfully, they invite you inside anyway.

They give you a tour of the house. But nothing inside really says "pirate" until you spot a model ship on the fireplace mantel in the living room. It looks almost as old as Blackbeard himself. Looking closer, it appears to be an exact replica of *Queen Anne's Revenge*.

You've got a pretty good eye for antiques. Working in the museum has definitely helped. This model ship appears valuable and could be loaded with clues. Is it possible that it was made for Blackbeard and these people happened to find it somewhere? You can't help but wonder if there's something on the boat that points to the treasure.

But you also remember the crawl space under the front porch. Could the treasure be under the house?

To ask to study the pirate ship for clues, turn to page 84.

To crawl under the porch to look for clues, turn to page 86.

You hate to admit it, but Cathy is right. You shouldn't just dig up historical land without permission. The two of you go to City Hall, fill out some forms, and meet with local officials about digging at the site.

They seem to like you and are impressed when you tell them about your museum. After a few days, you get the go-ahead to dig at the site. You just need to be respectful of the land. They'd also like you to share what you find.

"I'm not sure we'll find anything," you say. "But that sounds like a fair deal."

You shake hands, sign some documents, and head out to start digging.

You and Cathy return to the site and begin digging into the overgrown grass, careful not to disturb the foundation stones. You shovel the dirt onto a tarp, and Cathy picks through it for clues.

You both work hard most of the day but are disappointed not to find anything. Cathy decides to take a break and eat a donut. She is about as frustrated and wiped out as you are. You're thinking about having a treat yourself. But just then, you feel your shovel hit something hard.

To quit digging and search the coast instead, turn to page 88.

To investigate what you hit with the shovel, turn to page 90.

You're not happy about Cathy putting a stop to your search, but she's right. You can't just break the rules and dig wherever you like. Historical landmarks should be treated with respect. Knowing that, you're pretty sure the town won't give you permission to dig around the ruins of Blackbeard's old house.

Cathy says you could try taking tours of the town to get more information. You agree. Maybe it will lead to some clues about the pirate's treasure.

You go on several tours and learn a lot about the history of Bath. You even hear stories about Blackbeard and his partnership with Governor Charles Eden. Although the information is interesting, you don't learn any new clues.

At the end of the week, it's time to head back home. You can't help but feel like you made the wrong choice coming to North Carolina. You took in a lot of tourist attractions and made a friend in Cathy.

But you're no closer to finding pirate gold than when you started. All you ended up with was a cool Blackbeard T-shirt.

THE END

To follow another path, turn to page 11.
To learn more about Blackbeard, turn to page 101.

You want to study the model pirate ship. It's the next best thing to studying Blackbeard's actual ship. You ask Bill and Verna if you can borrow the ship to study it. They seem surprised. They aren't too thrilled by the idea and explain that it's very valuable. You offer them $2,000 and a promise to be very careful with it. They accept.

You carefully take the ship to your car and bring it into your hotel room. Using a strong magnifying glass, you study the ship very carefully. You're amazed by how much detail was put into the replica. There are forty guns, just like Blackbeard's ship. The masts and rigging seem accurate.

But as you scan across the underside of the ship, you notice three words that make your heart sink. Stamped into the wood are the words: *MADE IN CHINA*.

The ship isn't old after all. It was made in a factory, probably with thousands of others. You can't believe you were so easily fooled! Your coworkers at the museum would definitely be laughing at you right now.

Frustrated, you stand up quickly, and your shirt catches the ship's bowsprit. It crashes to the ground, breaking into several pieces. You just paid $2,000 for a manufactured trinket. That's it. No more treasure hunting for you. You're done.

THE END

To follow another path, turn to page 11.
To learn more about Blackbeard, turn to page 101.

It's a long shot, but there may be a clue to Blackbeard's treasure hidden under the front porch. Both Bill and Verna tell you the porch isn't hiding anything, but you're not sure you believe them. They just want the treasure for themselves! They think you're strange for asking but agree to let you check out the area.

You crawl through a small opening along the side of the porch and wiggle your way into the tight space. You find rocks, leaves, and dirt, but not much else. Determined to find *something*, you keep going, looking for any trace of a clue. As you squirm further beneath the porch, you realize you're stuck.

As you call for help, you hear something that makes you freeze with terror. A copperhead snake is slithering your way. You scream and the snake strikes, sinking its fangs right into your nose. Your skin burns, and your whole face feels like it's on fire. The snake releases its bite and slithers away.

A copperhead snake

Outside, you can hear Bill dial 911. You probably won't die from the bite, but the snake almost scared you to death. It's time to face facts. Your treasure hunt is over.

THE END

To follow another path, turn to page 11.
To learn more about Blackbeard, turn to page 101.

You look down to see you hit a small rock. You look up in frustration. You realize you're not going to find anything here.

You can't understand why Blackbeard wouldn't want to keep his gold close. Is it possible that it was already found, and no one bothered to tell the rest of the world? You hope not, but you don't think it's here in the ruins of his old home.

You spend a good chunk of time putting the dirt back into the hole and replacing the clumps of grass as best you can. You're very frustrated and about ready to give up on your quest.

But Cathy isn't ready to give up yet. She convinces you to search the area around where *Queen Anne's Revenge* ran aground. Maybe Blackbeard took a bunch of his treasure and hid it somewhere along the beach.

The two of you walk up and down the beach using your metal detector, but you find nothing except an old set of keys and part of a locket. You're beginning to think your dreams of finding the pirate's plunder are just that—a dream.

Maybe you should have spent your money on a trip to the Cayman Islands instead. It doesn't look like Blackbeard's treasure is in North Carolina.

THE END

To follow another path, turn to page 11.
To learn more about Blackbeard, turn to page 101.

Upon closer inspection you see that you hit a rock. It isn't too big, though. You convince Cathy to help you lift it up. Working together, you both manage to slip your fingers under it and pull it out. Surprisingly, it comes up easily.

But you find an even bigger surprise underneath the rock. Instead of more dirt, you find a wooden hatch.

"What do we have here?" you ask Cathy. She claps her hands with an excited look on her face.

You poke the wood with your finger and realize it is pretty rotten. You brush the dirt away and pull up the metal ring. With a groan, the hatch opens. Swiping the cobwebs away, you discover there's an old ladder leading down into the ground.

"Is this Blackbeard's basement?" you ask.

Cathy can't believe there's a basement beneath the foundation. There aren't many houses in North Carolina that have them. This makes you think you're on to something.

When you climb down, you discover there's a lot of water at the bottom. It's old and smells terrible down here. You can't help but wonder what's waiting in the dark.

You walk down a damp hallway and see a decorative door that looks like it's from a pirate ship. You try to open it, but the door seems to be locked. There's a large hole where you think the knob used to be.

To reach into the hole and try to pick the lock, turn to page 92.

To stick your flashlight into the hole, turn to page 94.

The excitement is almost too much to handle. You can't wait to open the door.

"I don't know if this is a great idea," Cathy says. She's looking at the door like it's an evil creature from the sea.

"It'll be fine," you insist and stick your hand in the hole.

Inside, you can feel a metal knob sticking up. You push it, certain that will undo the lock. But as you do, you hear a click. Then something heavy and sharp slams down on your wrist.

"It's not fine!" you cry out as pain tears through your body.

When you pull your arm back, you discover your hand has been chopped off! You quickly wrap up the stump to try to stop the bleeding. As Cathy takes you to the hospital, you wonder if they might give you a hook for a hand—just like a pirate.

THE END

To follow another path, turn to page 11.
To learn more about Blackbeard, turn to page 101.

Something doesn't feel right about putting your hand into a strange, creepy hole in a pirate's door. You've seen enough movies to know that pirate treasure is sometimes booby-trapped.

To play it safe, you stick your flashlight into the hole instead. You hear a small click and a loud clunk as something heavy drops onto your flashlight. The light goes dark, and you pull it out. You see that the end has been chopped off as the batteries dump out onto the floor.

"Yikes," you whisper to Cathy. "That could've been my hand."

You give the door a shove, and it moves. Springing the booby trap unlocked the door! The old hinges groan and squeak as the room is revealed. Inside, you see a huge pile of treasure. It's heaped almost to the ceiling, and you can't believe your eyes. You've found the treasure in Blackbeard's basement!

"We found it!" Cathy cries.

You cast the flashlight's beam across the mounds of riches to take in the sight. In front of you is the largest diamond you have ever seen. Cathy reaches for it, but you suddenly have a bad feeling.

To stop Cathy from grabbing the diamond, turn to page 96.

To let Cathy pick up the treasure, turn to page 98.

Something is telling you to be careful. You quickly grab Cathy's arm.

"No," you say. "Not yet, Cathy."

She looks confused. You explain that you have a bad feeling about the diamond, especially after the booby-trapped door. You both decide not to touch anything and slowly back away, leaving the treasure alone for now. You're nervous about leaving a fortune in treasure alone. Still, it's better to be safe than sorry.

When you reach the surface, you contact the authorities at City Hall. You let them know you've found the treasure, just as you agreed.

Within a few days they dig into the basement room from above and carefully remove every piece of treasure from the vault. When they try to grab the diamond, the basement vault's stone floor collapses. Far below is a deep, watery cave.

You and Cathy high-five. That could've been you, dropping into the chasm with the pirate's treasure.

Good work! You've discovered and saved Blackbeard's loot! You agree to share displaying the infamous pirate's bounty at your museum and with the North Carolina Museum of History.

THE END

To follow another path, turn to page 11.
To learn more about Blackbeard, turn to page 101.

You're probably just being paranoid. How many traps could the infamous pirate have left behind, anyway?

You decide to let Cathy pick up the diamond. As she grabs it, you can see it's attached to a thin black cord. As she pulls up on the jewel, you hear an ominous click.

"That doesn't sound good," Cathy says. She looks at you like she's done something wrong.

A second later, the stone floor drops out beneath the treasure hoard. The two of you quickly jump back into the hallway as the treasure plummets down into a dark, deep, watery cave.

"NO!" you shout in frustration. "You've got to be kidding me, Blackbeard!"

Your voice is almost lost in the noise of jewels, gold coins, and artifacts tumbling and splashing into the depths below. You watch helplessly as Blackbeard's fortune slips from your grasp. Sadly, you have no idea if you'll be able to find it down in the deep, dangerous pit.

Cathy looks at the diamond and shakes her head. She's not even sure it's real. You've found Blackbeard's treasure, but it's gotten away from you—for now.

THE END

To follow another path, turn to page 11.
To learn more about Blackbeard, turn to page 101.

Blackbeard in 1715

CHAPTER 5

A PIRATE'S LIFE AND DEATH

There are few pirates in history as famous, or infamous, as Blackbeard. Like many legends, stories of the pirate seem almost impossible to believe. The more people talked about him, the more frightening and dangerous he seemed to become. Was Blackbeard as bad as everyone thought he was? Or were the stories about him just tall tales?

Most experts think Edward Teach was born in 1680 in England. He served as a privateer for the British government from 1701–1713. After seeing the cargo he seized from ships in the West Indies go to others, Teach decided a pirate's life was the life for him.

Many believed Blackbeard set his dark beard on fire before battle. In truth, the pirate lit small candles and fuses and stuck them into his hat and beard. The smoke, along with his fierce eyes and thick beard, gave him an evil appearance that scared the crews of the ships he raided.

Another legend claimed that Blackbeard killed one of his crew members each day to keep the rest of them in line. But the truth was that Blackbeard likely didn't kill anyone until his final battle where he fought for his life.

Alexander Spotswood, governor of North Carolina, was determined to take care of the Blackbeard problem for good. He ordered a British naval force to attack the pirate and end his reign of terror. Blackbeard's end came at the hands of Lieutenant Robert Maynard on November 22, 1718.

In 1718, Blackbeard was defeated and killed on his ship, the *Adventure*, by British Lieutenant Robert Maynard.

In his final battle, Blackbeard was supposedly shot five times and stabbed more than twenty times with a sword. After being killed, he was beheaded and his body was thrown overboard.

But even death couldn't stop the dreaded pirate. Blackbeard's headless body supposedly swam around his ship three times before he stopped moving!

The story of Blackbeard's final swim is just a legend. But what is true is that his head was hung from the bowsprit of Maynard's ship.

Later, his head was displayed on a pole that overlooked the southern end of Chesapeake Bay. It was thought that the sight of the dead pirate's head would scare off any current or would-be pirates.

Blackbeard's legend reached far and wide and still lives to this day. It's hard to believe that he was a pirate for only a short time. Some historians believe Blackbeard ruled the seas for about two years.

Was Blackbeard as infamous and dangerous as people thought? The world may never know for sure!

Blackbeard Timeline

1680
Edward Teach is believed to have been born in Bristol, England.

Early 1700s
Teach serves as a privateer for the British government.

1716
Teach joins Benjamin Hornigold's crew as a pirate.

1717
Teach begins pirating on his own as Blackbeard after seizing a ship he later renames *Queen Anne's Revenge*.

Late 1717
Blackbeard meets and works with pirate Stede Bonnet.

May 1718
Blackbeard sets up a blockade of Charles Town, South Carolina, holding hostages and demanding medical supplies in exchange for the prisoners.

June 1718
Blackbeard is pardoned by Governor Charles Eden.

August 1718
Blackbeard returns to pirating and captures two French ships near Bermuda.

November 22, 1718
Blackbeard is killed and beheaded by Lieutenant Robert Maynard of the Royal Navy.

MORE PLUNDERING PIRATES

William Kidd, also known as Captain Kidd, was a Scottish sea captain. He became a pirate in 1697 and was hanged for murder and piracy in 1701.

Anne Bonny was an Irish pirate who caused trouble in the Caribbean. She is one of the few female pirates in known history. She was sentenced for execution in 1720 but was spared because she was pregnant. After being released from prison, she got married, had children and lived the rest of her days away from the pirate's life.

John Rackham, also known as Calico Jack, was an English pirate who operated in Cuba and the Bahamas in the 1700s. He fell in love with Anne Bonny, and together they raided ships along the coast of Jamaica.

Zheng Yi Sao was a Chinese pirate leader who plundered the South China Sea in the early 1800s. She married a pirate at a young age and took over his fleet when her husband died in 1807. She terrorized the coast of southern China where people were murdered, robbed, and sold into slavery.

Bartholomew Roberts, also known as Black Bart, was the most successful pirate of his time. His pirating rampage lasted from 1700 to 1725. It was believed he inspired many of the other pirates who terrorized the seven seas. He was killed in 1722, and his body was thrown overboard, as he'd requested from his crew.

Other Paths to Explore

>>> In your hunt for Blackbeard's treasure, you explored several areas looking for his riches. What would you bring along to ensure a successful adventure? Are there areas you wouldn't want to investigate? Are there any locations too dangerous for you to even consider checking out for yourself?

>>> To this day, Blackbeard's treasure hasn't been found. The wreckage of his most famous ship, *Queen Anne's Revenge,* was discovered, but there was no treasure anywhere in sight. Do you believe there's a big pile of gold from Blackbeard's pirating days hidden somewhere? Do you think it was already found by someone else? Where would you look that no one else has thought of?

>>> Some believe Governor Charles Eden and Blackbeard became friends after he was pardoned. Many believe Blackbeard paid off Eden to look the other way and ignore his crimes. Do you think it's possible the treasure was hidden somewhere on Eden's estate? Why might Governor Eden take gold that was stolen from others?

BIBLIOGRAPHY

"7 Places Blackbeard's Gold Could've Been Stashed," Mental Floss.com, September 20, 2015, https://www.mentalfloss.com/article/68887/7-places-blackbeards-gold-couldve-been-stashed

"Blackbeard," *Encyclopedia Britannica*, August 22, 2022, https://www.britannica.com/biography/Blackbeard.

"Blackbeard Killed Off North Carolina," History.com, November 19, 2020, https://www.history.com/this-day-in-history/blackbeard-killed-off-north-carolina.

"Did Archaeologists Uncover Blackbeard's Treasure?" by Abigail Tucker, *Smithsonian Magazine*, March 2011, https://www.smithsonianmag.com/history/did-archaeologists-uncover-blackbeards-treasure-215890/.

"Does Blackbeard's Treasure Actually Exist, or Is It Just a Legend Seen Only in Movies?" by Lianna Tedesco, *The Travel*, October 24, 2020, https://www.thetravel.com/where-is-blackbeards-treasure/.

"Uncovering the Truth Behind the Legends of Blackbeard," by Sophie Olver, *Culture Trip*, June 5, 2018, https://theculturetrip.com/europe/united-kingdom/england/articles/uncovering-the-truth-behind-the-legends-of-blackbeard/.

GLOSSARY

bowsprit (BOH-sprit)—a long pole that extends from the front of a ship and holds the front sails

galleon (GAH-lee-uhn)—a large, square-rigged sailing ship often used by Spain from the 1400s to the 1700s

gorge (GORJ)—a canyon with steep walls that rise straight upward

landlubber (LAND-luh-buhr)—an unseasoned sailor or someone unfamiliar with the sea

paranoid (PAIR-uh-noyd)—fearful or suspicious that someone means to harm you

pardon (PAHR-duhn)—an official act of forgiveness for a serious offense or crime

privateer (prye-vuh-TEER)—a person who owns a ship and is permitted by the government to attack and steal from enemy ships

rigging (RIH-ging)—ropes and chains used to support the masts and work the sails on a ship

stalactite (stuh-LAK-tahyt)—a rocky formation that hangs from the ceiling of a cave and is created by dripping water

stalagmite (stuh-LAG-mahyt)—a rocky formation that stands on the floor of a cave and is created by drips of water from above

READ MORE

Fox, E. T. *Pirates*. New York: DK Publishing, 2017.

Hoena, B. A. *Blackbeard: Captain of the Queen Anne's Revenge*. Minneapolis: Bellwether Media, Inc., 2021.

O'Donnell, Liam. *Hop on the Pirate History Boat*. Chicago: Heinemann-Raintree, 2018.

Vonne, Mira. *Gross Facts About Pirates*. North Mankato, MN: Capstone Publishing, 2017.

INTERNET SITES

History of Pirates
mocomi.com/history-of-pirates/

Pirates
dkfindout.com/us/history/pirates/

Pirates, Privateers, Corsairs, Buccaneers: What's the Difference?
britannica.com/story/pirates-privateers-corsairs-buccaneers-whats-the-difference

ABOUT THE AUTHOR

Thomas Kingsley Troupe is the author of more than 200 books for young readers. He's written books about everything from third grade werewolves to ballerinas to talking spaceships. He's even written a book about dirt. Thomas wrote his first book when he was in second grade and has been making up stories ever since. When he's not behind the keyboard, he enjoys reading, playing video games, and hunting ghosts with the Twin Cities Paranormal Society. Otherwise, he's probably taking a nap or something. Thomas lives in Woodbury, Minnesota, with his two sons.